Withdrawn

W9-BKR-691

The Gifts of the Nativity

Written by Jeana James   Illustrated by Sarah C. Nightingale

CFI • An Imprint of Cedar Fort, Inc.
Springville, Utah

The Beautiful Nativity Scene

is a tradition that celebrates the miracle of Christ's birth. The glorious meaning of the Nativity is a reminder of the eternal gifts Jesus Christ gives to each of us, for He is the center and true meaning of Christmas.

Have you ever thought about what each piece of the *Nativity* means in your own life?

Think of the stable as representing the protection of your heavenly and earthly parents, just as the stable protected the baby Jesus.

Heavenly Father gives us commandments that provide safety, peace, and happiness if we choose to obey. Earthly parents likewise shelter, love, and nurture us. Loving parents are a great gift from God.

At the birth of Christ, the Lord sent *angels* to announce the glorious event.

Today, *angels* minister, protect, and deliver God's messages. They bring peace and comfort to us, especially during times of need.

The *angels* represent ALL OF US, since we each were part of the joyous celebration! We had longed for the day, waiting for the night our Savior was born.

The donkey is known for
steadiness and strength.
It carried Mary to Bethlehem, making
the journey easier for her.

Are we willing to carry the burden of others
and help them on their way?
As we unselfishly serve and lift others,
we bring the true spirit of
Christ into *Christmas.*

Humble animals

shared their manger with the
Son of God at His birth.

Mary and Joseph

must have realized how blessed they were to be sheltered with the *animals,* rather than being out in the cold. When we find ourselves in such humble circumstances, we too should be grateful, appreciating every sweet blessing we have.

The shepherds
carefully watched
and *cared* for their fold.

They followed that one
bright star to
Bethlehem and to the

Baby Jesus

on that first
Christmas night.

*Known for its endurance
and strength, the camel*
escorted the wise men to witness the Christ child.
The *camel* reminds us that we should press
forward on our journey to the Savior.

Day by day, we pray for the strength to move forward and live righteously so that we will arrive where we want to be—in the presence of our *Lord.*

The Wise Men

were not ordinary men. They were chosen to witness the arrival of the Son of God to the earth. They could see the star when others could not. They traveled long and far to witness the beautiful sight of the Christ child.

Our life is like

the Wise Men's journey.

It will be long and hard at times, but in the end we will be with our Savior forever. If we open our heart to Him, He will guide and direct us.

The Wise Men

brought priceless and precious gifts of

gold, frankincense, and myrrh.

These *treasures* were the best they had to give, and each gift testified of the divinity of the Savior.

Gold, incorruptible and shining, symbolized Christ's status as the Son of God. The *frankincense* was a fragrant type of incense that was burned in the temple during sacrifice. This gift symbolized Christ's role as the Savior of the world. And *myrrh* is described as the oil of Resurrection and symbolized Christ's victory over death.

Like *the Wise Men,* we want to give our best gifts to our Savior to honor Him. To do this, we keep His commandments, serve others, and always remember Him.

Joseph

was a humble carpenter—*diligent*, *hardworking*, and *careful*. When he was called by God to be the earthly father of the newborn King, Joseph rose to the occasion. He served his wife and child and protected them through the Lord's guidance. He did not shirk the *responsibility* that was placed on him; he did his best to perform God's will.

We too must be prepared to accept the responsibilities that God will give us on this earth. Are we ready?

Mary was highly favored of *God* because of her *righteousness, goodness,* and *purity.* Because she was so fair and righteous, she was called to bear and raise the Son of God.

Mary was obedient to the Lord; she raised Jesus and loved Him. Like the love of Mary, God's love for us is deep and abiding, but on an infinitely larger scale. He loves all of His children unconditionally, and because of this He sent His Son to redeem us all.

The Baby Jesus is the most significant of all.

His birth is the center of the beautiful Nativity and of our *salvation*. He came to Earth to save us all, to redeem us from sin and pain. He descended below all things so that we could rise above. He is the Light of the World. Every day, He calls to us and invites us to come unto Him. For His way is the way to *salvation*. He gives us hope that we can one day return to live with our Heavenly Father.

The *Nativity* as a whole depicts a family—father, mother, Son. Just as Christ is at the center of the Nativity, the family is at the center of Christmas.

When we put *Christ* at the center of our families, our homes will be filled with peace, joy, happiness, and light all year long.

The *Stable's* protection.

The *Angels'* peace and comfort.

The *Donkey's* steadiness and strength.

The *Animals'* humility.

The *Shepherds,* who followed the light.

The *Camel* that pressed forward.

The *Wise Men's* best gifts.

Joseph, who did his best to perform God's will.

Mary, who was so fair and righteous.

Jesus, who gives us hope.

References

(Luke 2:7) And she brought forth her firstborn son, and wrapped him in swaddling clothes, and laid him in a manger; because there was no room for them in the inn.

(Luke 2:10, 13–14) And the angel said unto them, Fear not: for, behold, I bring you good tidings of great joy, which shall be to all people. . . . And suddenly there was with the angel a multitude of the heavenly host praising God, and saying, Glory to God in the highest, and on earth peace, good will toward men.

(Luke 2:32) A light to lighten the Gentiles, and the glory of thy people Israel.

(Luke 2:12) And this shall be a sign unto you; Ye shall find the babe wrapped in swaddling clothes, lying in a manger.

(Isaiah 1:3) The ox knoweth his owner, and the ass his master's crib: but Israel doth not know, my people doth not consider.

(Luke 2:8–10, 15–16, 20) And there were in the same country shepherds abiding in the field, keeping watch over their flock by night. And, lo, the angel of the Lord came upon them, and the glory of the Lord shone round about them: and they were sore afraid. . . . And the angel said unto them, Fear not: for, behold, I bring you good tidings of great joy, which shall be to all people. And it came to pass, as the angels were gone away from them into heaven, the shepherds said one to another, Let us now go even unto Bethlehem, and see this thing which is come to pass, which the Lord hath made known unto us. And they came with haste, and found Mary, and Joseph, and the babe lying in a manger. . . . And the shepherds returned, glorifying and praising God for all the things that they had heard and seen, as it was told unto them.

(Matthew 1:21) And she shall bring forth a son, and thou shalt call his name Jesus: for he shall save his people from their sins.

(Matthew 2:1–2) Now when Jesus was born in Bethlehem of Judæa in the days of Herod the king, behold, there came wise men from the east to Jerusalem, Saying, Where is he that is born King of the Jews? For we have seen his star in the east, and are come to worship him.

(Matthew 2:10–11) When they saw the star, they rejoiced with exceeding great joy. And when they were come into the house, they saw the young child with Mary his mother, and fell down, and worshipped him: and when they had opened their treasures, they presented unto him gifts; gold, and frankincense, and myrrh.

(Matthew 2:9) When they had heard the king, they departed; and, lo, the star, which they saw in the east, went before them, till it came and stood over where the young child was.

(Matthew 1:20, 24) But while he thought on these things, behold, the angel of the Lord appeared unto him in a dream, saying, Joseph, thou son of David, fear not to take unto thee Mary thy wife: for that which is conceived in her is of the Holy Ghost. . . . Then Joseph being raised from sleep did as the angel of the Lord had bidden him, and took unto him his wife.

(Luke 1:28, 30–31) And the angel came in unto her, and said, Hail, thou that art highly favoured, the Lord is with thee: blessed art thou among women. . . . And the angel said unto her, Fear not, Mary: for thou hast found favour with God. And, behold, though shalt conceive in thy womb, and bring forth a son, and shalt call his name Jesus.

(Luke 2:19) But Mary kept all these things, and pondered them in her heart.

(Matthew 1:21) And she shall bring forth a son, and thou shalt call his name Jesus: for he shall save his people from their sins.

(Luke 2:11, 14) For unto you is born this day in the city of David a Saviour, which is Christ the Lord. . . . Glory to God in the highest, and on earth peace, good will toward men.

(Luke 2:40) And the child grew, and waxed strong in spirit, filled with wisdom: and the grace of God was upon him.

I would like to dedicate this book to every child, young and old, who has gazed in awe at the Nativity, knowing that this beautiful miracle happened for each of us.

Jeana James

To my baby boy, our son, George, because we were always in it together; to my husband, Alex, because you're my rock and my world; to my family, because you were all there for us. And to my Heavenly Father and my Savior who have blessed us with so much.

Sarah C. Nightingale

Text © 2017 Jeana James
Illustrations © 2017 Sarah C. Nightingale
All rights reserved.

This is not an official publication of The Church of Jesus Christ of Latter-day Saints. The opinions and views expressed herein belong solely to the author and do not necessarily represent the opinions or views of Cedar Fort, Inc. Permission for the use of sources, graphics, and photos is also solely the responsibility of the author.

ISBN 13: 978-1-4621-2060-4

Published by CFI, an imprint of Cedar Fort, Inc.
2373 W. 700 S., Springville, UT 84663
Distributed by Cedar Fort, Inc., www.cedarfort.com

Library of Congress Control Number: 2017945319

Cover design and typesetting by Shawnda T. Craig & Kinsey Beckett
Cover design © 2017 Cedar Fort, Inc.
Edited by Chelsea Holdaway

Printed in the United States of America

10 9 8 7 6 5 4 3 2 1

Printed on acid-free paper